IDENTITY AND CIVIL RIGHTS

BY JIM OLLHOFF

VISIT US AT
WWW.ABDOPUBLISHING.COM

Published by ABDO Publishing Company, 8000 West 78th Street, Suite 310, Edina, MN 55439. Copyright ©2012 by Abdo Consulting Group, Inc. International copyrights reserved in all countries. No part of this book may be reproduced in any form without written permission from the publisher. ABDO & Daughters™ is a trademark and logo of ABDO Publishing Company.

Printed in the United States of America, North Mankato, Minnesota.
052011
092011

PRINTED ON RECYCLED PAPER

Editor: John Hamilton
Graphic Design: Sue Hamilton
Cover Design: Neil Klinepier
Cover Photo: Corbis
Interior Photos and Illustrations: Ancestry.com-pg 7; AP-pgs 28 & 29; Bancroft Library-pg 9; Corbis-pgs 15, 16 (left), 19 (top), 19 (bottom right), 25 & 27; Division of Rare and Manuscript Collections Cornell University-pg 16 (right); Getty Images-pgs 4, 5, 18 & 19 (bottom left) & 22; John Hamilton-pg 10; Granger Collection-pgs 17 & 26; Library of Congress-pgs 6, 12, 13, 14, 20 & 21; National Geographic-pg 8; Negative 050332 Courtesy Museum of New Mexico-pg 18; Wikipedia-pg 26

Library of Congress Cataloging-in-Publication Data

Ollhoff, Jim, 1959-
  Identity and civil rights / Jim Ollhoff.
    p. cm. -- (Hispanic American history)
  Includes index.
  ISBN 978-1-61783-057-0
  1. Hispanic Americans--History--19th century--Juvenile literature. 2. Hispanic Americans--History--20th century--Juvenile literature. 3. Spaniards--United States--History--19th century--Juvenile literature. 4. Spaniards--United States--History--20th century--Juvenile literature. I. Title.
  E184.S75O46 2012
  305.8968'073--dc23
                    2011018225

CONTENTS

Spanish explorer Gaspar de Portola's expedition spies San Francisco Bay and the Pacific Coast in 1769.

BECOMING AMERICAN

Beginning in the 1500s, Spain's empire in North America stretched from Florida to California. Many of the cities we know today, such as Santa Fe, San Francisco, and San Diego, began as Spanish forts, missions, and trading centers. The city of St. Augustine, Florida, was founded more than 50 years before the *Mayflower* brought Pilgrims to the East Coast.

However, in the 1800s, the Spanish Empire began to crumble. One by one, countries in South America declared their independence from Spain. Mexico won its independence in 1821.

The Mexican-American War was fought between 1846 and 1848. The war ended with a large amount of territory given to the United States. This territory included California, Nevada, Utah, and parts of Wyoming, Colorado, Arizona, and New Mexico. The 80,000 Hispanic people living in those territories instantly became American citizens.

In 1898, the United States fought a brief war with Spain. After a crushing defeat, Spain surrendered the Philippines, Cuba, Guam, and Puerto Rico to the United States. The Hispanic people in those islands became part of the American territories.

By 1898, the age of the Spanish Empire was officially over. However, a new age of Hispanic culture was beginning. In the 1900s, Latinos helped build a strong America. They worked in factories and fields. They worked as writers and artists. They worked as scientists and doctors. Latinos became great leaders.

Twentieth-century America often didn't deal honorably with minority groups. Latinos faced racism and prejudice, and sometimes a loss of their civil rights. But courageous leaders defended Hispanic culture and helped push a vision for a diverse America, where all people could live together in peace.

Hispanic Americans during a celebration in Taos, New Mexico, in July 1940.

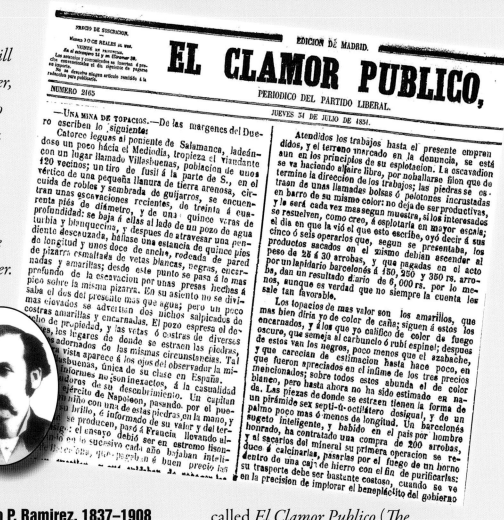

When still a teenager, Francisco Ramirez founded the first Spanish-language newspaper.

Francisco P. Ramirez, 1837–1908

Francisco P. Ramirez's grandfather came to Southern California in 1794. Francisco was born in 1837, and grew up as Los Angeles was becoming an important city. By the time he was 14, he was fluent in three languages: Spanish, English, and French.

When he was 17 years old, he founded a Spanish newspaper called *El Clamor Publico* (*The Public Outcry*). It was the first and only Spanish-language newspaper of the time, and became an important force that unified Hispanic people. As the newspaper grew, it became a strong voice as a defender of Hispanic people and culture. Francisco P. Ramirez was a courageous and intellectual leader who helped bring a sense of unity to Hispanic people.

SETTLING THE SOUTHWEST

A cattle drive across New Mexico.

Mexican cowboys were called vaqueros, and they were working in the American Southwest in the early 1600s. The vaqueros were expert horsemen. They worked to drive herds of cattle from one place to another. The vaqueros were gallant and tough, and proud of their skills.

As Americans began to develop a taste for beef, they needed larger and larger herds of cattle. More European-Americans came to the South and West, and became known as cowboys. The cowboys learned their skills from the vaqueros.

The vaqueros and cowboys took their herds over long distances. However, after the Civil War (1861-1865), large areas of land became private property. The invention of barbed wire made long cattle drives much more difficult.

A vaquero on a California ranch.

Today, the skills of the vaqueros are celebrated in the rodeo. Rodeo is a Spanish word for "surround," as in the pen that surrounds a bull. In the days of the Old West in the mid-1800s, cowboy ranch hands sometimes gathered and competed to see who had the best style when it came to riding untrained horses. When they were on the trail, vaqueros and cowboys often had to rope and tie down sick calves for medical treatment. Both of these activities can be seen in modern rodeos. Rodeos today feature skills such as horse riding, bull riding, roping, and steer wrestling. Modern rodeo riders can thank the vaqueros for handing down these skills!

Modern rodeo riders use the skills that working vaqueros practiced in the 1800s.

Rafael Chacón, 1833–1925

Jose Rafael Sotero Chacón was born in 1833 in Santa Fe, in today's state of New Mexico. He attended military school, and eventually found himself in the United States military during the wars with the Native Americans in the American Southwest. In 1861, he was ordered to report to the Union military to fight in the Civil War, in a unit under the command of frontiersman Kit Carson. Chacón was a brave and clever military man, and eventually became a major in the United States Army. He was known as an honest man who proudly said, "I am poor, and my only inheritance is my honor." After he retired from the military, he served in the territorial legislature of New Mexico. When he was older, he wrote down his history, his stories, and the experiences he had. Today, historians treasure his work as one of the few historical documents of the era that is told from a Hispanic point of view.

THE MEXICAN REVOLUTION

Porfirio Díaz

In the years leading up to 1910, the economic climate in Mexico grew worse and worse. The rich people were getting richer, and the poor were getting poorer. The dictatorship of President Porfirio Díaz hurt the working class and the majority of Mexican citizens. Many different groups were either seeking power for themselves or trying to help the growing numbers of poverty-stricken Mexican citizens. Finally, the Mexican people had enough. In 1910, a revolution exploded in Mexico, and the government of Porfirio Díaz began to collapse.

For the next 10 years, chaos and lawlessness were common. Desperados, criminals who rode in gangs, terrorized the countryside.

During much of this time, the European nations were fighting World War I (1914-1918). The United States was afraid that Germany would take advantage of the chaos in Mexico and use the country as a base to launch attacks. The United States Navy blockaded Mexico, making the internal Mexican problems even worse.

The Mexican people suffered terribly during this time. About 700,000 Mexicans fled the chaos. They crossed the Rio Grande, a river which forms part of the border between Mexico and the United States. They tried to find a better life in the United States.

General Francisco "Pancho" Villa (center) was a famous Mexican revolutionary. He created and led a large army against the rule of President Porfirio Díaz and wealthy Mexican landowners.

MIGRATION TO THE UNITED STATES

Mexican laborers were employed to harvest carrots, cotton, pecans, sugar beets, and many other crops.

Mexican citizens crossed the border into the United States in great numbers during the Mexican Revolution of 1910 to 1920. The border was mostly unguarded, so people could cross into the United States without being stopped. Hispanics began to get jobs in the United States, where they often worked for very low wages. Usually, their jobs were ones that United States citizens didn't want.

Many of these new immigrants couldn't speak English. They were often taken advantage of by cheating employers. Sometimes they were forced to live in poverty-stricken areas with hundreds of other Hispanic people. These areas were often called barrios.

George Santayana (1863–1952)

George Santayana was a philosopher and a writer. He was born in Spain and grew up in the United States. He taught at Harvard University. He is considered by many to be one of the most important philosophers of the twentieth century. He is famous for saying, "Those who do not remember the past are condemned to repeat it." This is a reminder to study and learn from history, so that we do not make the same mistakes over and over again.

HELPING BUILD A STRONG AMERICA

Hispanic immigrants had great obstacles to overcome, including racism, poverty, and learning the English language. Despite these problems, many Hispanic people created better lives for themselves, and helped build a stronger United States.

Louis Agassiz Fuertes (1874–1927) was a bird expert. He drew and painted his subjects with amazing detail. In 1899, he accompanied an elite group of scientists on the Harriman Expedition to explore Alaska. Later, he taught at Cornell University in New York.

Carlos Finlay

Doctors give each other shots to prevent yellow fever.

Carlos Finlay (1833–1915) and Juan Guiteras (1852–1925) were both Cuban doctors. They helped discover the cause of yellow fever, a disease that killed tens of thousands of people each year. By working to eliminate the mosquito that caused yellow fever, they were able to save countless people from terrible suffering.

Carlos Finlay

Juan Guiteras

Ezequiel
Cabeza
de Baca

Ezequiel Cabeza de Baca (1864–1917) was born in New Mexico, and studied to become a journalist. He helped publish a Spanish weekly newspaper. He was elected the second governor of New Mexico in 1916, but unfortunately died a year later after an illness.

Luis Muñoz Rivera

Luis Muñoz Marin

Luis Muñoz Rivera (1859–1916) was a Puerto Rican poet and writer. He became a political leader, speaking out for the independence of Puerto Rico. He worked hard for the people of the Caribbean island. His son, **Luis Muñoz Marin (1898-1980),** would become the first democratically elected governor of Puerto Rico in 1949.

A mural by Diego Rivera shows scenes from the Mexican Revolution.

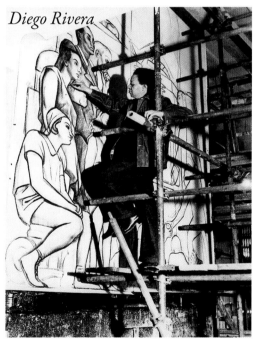

Diego Rivera

Frida Kahlo

Diego Rivera (1886–1957) was a Mexican artist who helped popularize the mural, which is artwork that is painted directly on a wall. Rivera painted murals in Mexico, San Francisco, New York, and Detroit. He was married to another Mexican artist, **Frida Kahlo (1907-1954).**

THE GREAT DEPRESSION

In the 1920s, the economy of the United States was good, World War I was over, and things seemed to be looking up. Then, the stock market crashed in 1929. Within a very short time, about 13 million Americans lost their jobs. The Great Depression was a terrible time in the United States, with too many people searching for too few jobs. Even those who had jobs saw their pay cut drastically. Many people could not feed their families.

Many places where Latinos worked closed, including steel mills, manufacturing plants, factories, and farms.

Cattle ranchers laid off thousands of workers because they could no longer afford to pay them.

In bad times, people naturally look for someone to blame. Some people said the Great Depression was the fault of Hispanic immigrants. They believed that immigrants were taking most of the available jobs. This wasn't true, but people were anxious to believe anything that would give them a reason for their misery. A movement grew to pressure the government to send Mexican immigrants back to Mexico. This was called the Mexican Repatriation.

A Mexican field worker beside his home at the edge of a field. During the Great Depression, many people traveled across the country to find work.

In the 1930s, both legal and illegal Hispanic immigrants were deported to Mexico.

At first, only illegal immigrants were deported to Mexico. But soon, Hispanic people in general were also targeted. Even Hispanic families who had lived in the United States for generations became victims of repatriation.

During the 1930s, about a half-million Hispanic people—illegal and legal immigrants—were deported to Mexico. It was a terrible injustice done to these families. It was an act born out of fear, hate, and desperation. It created much anger and resentment for years to come.

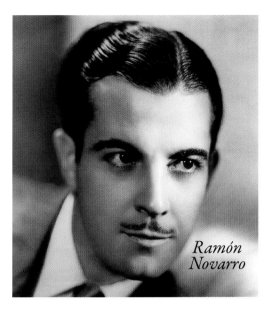

Ramón Novarro

Even during the Great Depression, some Hispanics succeeded in creating great things. One such person was **Ramón Novarro (1899–1968)**. He was one of the most popular Hollywood actors in the days of silent films. Silent films were created before the technology was available to include sound in films. Novarro is famous for his lead role in the film *Ben Hur*.

Ramón Novarro played the lead character Judah Ben-Hur in the 1925 film *Ben-Hur*.

A HERO GOES TO WASHINGTON

Dennis Chavez (1888-1962) was a hero who overcame huge challenges and inspired untold numbers of people. He was the first Hispanic to serve an entire term as a United States senator. He continued to be reelected throughout a long career.

Dennis Chavez was born in 1888 in New Mexico. In 1917, he was offered a job with a senator as an assistant executive clerk. He moved to Washington DC, where he worked in the Senate during the day and went to college at night to become a lawyer.

Chavez was elected to the New Mexico state legislature in 1922. In 1930 and 1932, he was elected to the United States House of Representatives. He then went on to become a senator, a position he held for the rest of his life. He wasn't the first Hispanic senator. Octaviano Larrazolo held that honor, but he was elected to fill an unexpired term. Dennis Chavez was elected to a whole term. Further, he was reelected four times. Chavez died in 1962, during his fifth term as senator. Vice President Lyndon Johnson spoke at Chavez's funeral.

Chavez gave great inspiration to Americans, who saw him as an effective leader and politician. Because of courageous people like Dennis Chavez, the path for Hispanic Americans today can lead anywhere.

Dennis Chavez became the U.S. senator from New Mexico in 1935. He was reelected to the office four times, remaining in office until his death in 1962.

WORLD WAR II

On December 7, 1941, Japanese forces attacked the United States military base at Pearl Harbor, Hawaii. The sneak attack forced the United States to enter World War II. It declared war on Japan and Germany, and began a four-year struggle to end tyranny in Europe and Asia.

Approximately 250,000 to 500,000 Hispanic Americans bravely fought in World War II. The exact number is unknown because records were not kept on who was Hispanic and who was not. For many Hispanics, joining the war effort was a way to escape prejudice. They were proud patriots who fought bravely for their country. Several were awarded the Medal of Honor, the highest military decoration awarded by the United States.

Japanese attack on Pearl Harbor, December 7, 1941.

Lucian Adams was one of several Hispanic Americans who were awarded the Medal of Honor for service in World War II.

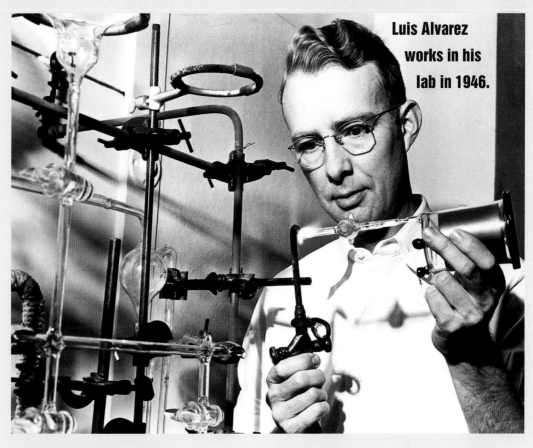

Luis Alvarez works in his lab in 1946.

Luis Alvarez (1911–1988)

Luis Alvarez was a nuclear physicist and an inventor. Sometimes he is called "the Thomas Edison of the Atomic Age." Born in San Francisco, California, he attended college at the University of Chicago. He discovered important facts about cosmic rays, and then began to study subatomic particles. He also studied radioactivity. During World War II, he used his knowledge of radioactivity to help develop the nuclear bomb. He also helped invent several radar systems.

In 1968, Alvarez won the Nobel Prize in Physics, an award given once a year to a physicist who has made great discoveries or contributions to physics.

In 1980, Alvarez and his son put forth the idea that the dinosaurs were killed off when an asteroid collided with Earth. It is a theory that is still debated today.

A young Hispanic man in a zoot suit.

Torn clothing on victims of a "zoot suit riot."

On the home front, the struggle for civil rights continued. Hispanic youth became the target of prejudice and hatred during what was called the "zoot suit riots." Zoot suits were a style of clothing in the 1930s and 1940s. A zoot suit consisted of a pair of high-waisted, wide-legged pants, and a long coat with pads in the shoulders. It was popular among African Americans and Mexican Americans, and was popular in England. In 1943, Mexican youth in Los Angeles wearing zoot suits became victims of assaults by military soldiers. The zoot suit riots briefly spread to other cities.

World War II ended in 1945. When Hispanic soldiers returned home, they often faced the same discrimination and prejudice as before. In many cases, however, Hispanic soldiers were honored for service to their country. The struggle for Hispanic American identity and civil rights continued.

On June 25, 1969, Pancho Gonzales competed against Charles Pasarell (not shown) at England's Wimbledon Championships. The 2-day, 183-game match was the longest one ever played at Wimbledon at the time. Gonzales won.

Pancho Gonzales, 1928–1995

Ricardo "Pancho" Gonzales was a tennis player who won more championships in the 1950s and early 1960s than anyone else of that era. He was born in Los Angeles, California, the son of Mexican immigrants. He taught himself how to play tennis by watching others, and then by practicing long and hard. He became known for his speed and agility, but especially his dogged determination on the court. Being one of the first Hispanic tennis players, he had to fight prejudice as well as opponents on the tennis court. He was a fearsome player and a colorful personality. He died of cancer in 1995.

GLOSSARY

CIVIL RIGHTS

The rights that individuals have, including the right to not be harassed by the government or private organizations. These often include the right to vote, the right to a fair trial, and the right to equal treatment.

CIVIL WAR

The war fought between America's Northern and Southern states from 1861-1865. The Southern states were for slavery. They wanted to start their own country. Northern states fought against slavery and a division of the country.

GREAT DEPRESSION

The Great Depression was a period of severe economic downturn, starting in 1929 and lasting about a decade. During the Great Depression, jobs were scarce, manufacturing plants were closed, and few people had extra money.

IMMIGRANT

A person who has entered a country intending to live there permanently.

MEXICAN-AMERICAN WAR

In 1845, the independent Republic of Texas became a part of the United States. This angered Mexico, which considered Texas a part of its territory. The United States and Mexico also clashed over control of California. These conflicts led to war between the two countries, which lasted from 1846 until 1848.

Mexican Repatriation

The mass deportation of hundreds of thousands of legal and illegal immigrants to Mexico during the 1930s.

Nobel Prize

An award given out each year to someone who has made important achievements in a particular area of study. There are six awards: chemistry, physics, physiology/medicine, literature, economics, and peace.

Radar

A way to find planes, ships and other objects. Radar stands for <u>ra</u>dio <u>d</u>etection <u>an</u>d <u>r</u>anging. The system sends out high-frequency electromagnetic waves, which bounce off any objects they hit, reflecting back to the source.

Radioactivity

A stream of particles that emits from a source such as uranium. This energy can cause sickness or be fatal to people who are exposed to the radiation.

Vaqueros

Hispanic cowboys who managed large herds of cattle before most European-American cowboys came to the Southwest.

World War I

A war that was fought in Europe from 1914 to 1918, involving countries around the world. The United States entered the war in April 1917.

World War II

A conflict across the world, lasting from 1939-1945. The United States entered the war in December 1941.

Zoot Suit Riots

A series of attacks in 1943 by American servicemen on American Hispanic youth wearing zoot suits, a particular style of clothing.

INDEX